I0461934

Corporate Cornerstone

Volume Two

—

A collection of Marketing and Business essays for the successful professional.

—

By Christopher Melotti

Book cover art by Christopher Melotti
PhotoID 41108503 @Rawpixelimages | Dreamstime.com

Australia
First Date of Publish: 1 April, 2017

C. N. Melotti (Author Website)
www.cnmelotti.com

Melotti Media
www.melottimedia.com.au

Contents Page

Preface from the Author

About This Book's Content

In today's face-paced and complex business environment, it is highly advantageous for everyone within the corporate world to have a comfortable understanding of *all* of the active functions and departments in an organisation. It allows the bigger picture to be seen when undertaking strategic decisions, which can ultimately affect the success of that organisation.

One such function is that of Marketing: the churning turbine that aims to devise strategy and implement tactics to connect a business to its customers to generate results. Marketing is a versatile, crucial and ever-changing practise that is often unfortunately misunderstood or underappreciated, but also one with unlimited depth and infinite purposes. Customers and markets today are volatile, highly educated and evolving every minute of the day with shifting dynamics, demands, demographics and dimensions. The Marketing department of an organisation must always be moving at an equally high speed to ensure it can answer such a demanding call to not only research and understand the market, but make effective and efficient strategic decisions which will ultimately determine how a business becomes and remains successful.

The Corporate Cornerstone volumes are designed as a brief collection of Marketing and Business essays for the successful business professional looking to further their knowledge. The volumes will be released regularly with fresh and informative topics.

This book differs from average business non-fiction publications, as I wrote it to be a summarised, easy-to-read guide which can be easily absorbed by all readers: from the student seeking an alternative resource, to the corporate professional looking to further their knowledge.

I hope you get as much out of reading this as I did writing it.

About The Author: Christopher Melotti

My name is Christopher Melotti, and I am a
Professional Copywriter, Marketer and
Author from Australia.

I am the owner and founder of Melotti Media,
where
I offer freelance Marketing consultancy and
Copywriting services to a diverse range of
organisations and clients.

I hold a *Bachelor of Commerce and
Marketing Degree* and a *Masters Degree in
Commercial Law*, both from Macquarie
University in Australia.

I have been a Marketing Practitioner for over ten years, spanning
Hospitality, Fast Moving Consumer Goods (FMCG), Medical Devices,
Pharmaceutical, Healthcare and Property industries. In addition, I have
Marketing Creative Agency experience and teach regular classes on
Marketing and Copywriting with organisations such as General Assembly.

I hold the prestigious title of *Certified Practising Marketer* (CPM) and am
currently an active and contributing member of the Australian Marketing
Institute (AMI), achieving the National Finalist in the AMI's *Award for
Marketing Excellence* in both 2013 and 2014, Finalist for the AMI's *Young
Future Leader Award* in 2013 and 2014 and won it in 2015, for outstanding
contributions to the Marketing Field, volunteer work and further Marketing
education.

I thoroughly enjoy expressing creativity and passing on my knowledge, to
which my published books are a testament to. Thank you for sharing your
valuable time with me, and I hope the following pages help you learn and
evolve your career!

Christopher Melotti BComm:Mtkg, MCommLaw, AMAMI CPM

Marketing Digitally At Close Proximity

It's all about physical location, and the Marketer's ability to digitally enhance local communications in real time.

The digital platform world is evolving at such a rapid pace today that there is no telling where it will head next or who will use it in the most unique way. Location-Based Marketing Technology and Proximity Marketing are both certainly on the rise.

As an umbrella term, Location-Based Marketing Technology is all about reaching potential customers within a specific physical space and pushing contextually relevant communications that are accessible in their local area which may be of interest them.

For example, the new iBeacon device works by sending out a Bluetooth Low Energy signal inside a bricks and mortar shop, designed to communicate with specific SmartPhone apps. These apps may react to the localised signal and let the customer know of specific discounts or new products in store that they should check out.

As a secondary use, it provides these locations with analytics of how many devices the Beacon has communicated with, and can be used for more innovative applications like directional messages, check-in prompts, local event reminders and even access pass payments.

Another example are Radio Frequency Identification (RFID) tags, which are electronic barcodes which can interact, via tiny antennae, with a localised network that can track them. This can be utilised as simply as placing these tags on in-store products which will automatically send the bill to your phone, thus bypassing the need for check-out lines, or more innovatively, such as placing them on conference and event wristbands which react to certain pieces of technology within the pavilion for a scavenger hunt, or allow the sharing of an experience online.

This kind of technology introduces a real paradigm shift in the way brands communicate with people, given that it integrates the digital world with the physical world closely, providing a very interactive and convenient experience (if utilised well). The ability of Location-Based Marketing Technology allows for targeting at the point of actual engagement and is a favourable balance between personalised and automated customer service.

Proximity marketing will give rise to a greater focus on:

(1) Mobile Device ordering
(2) Connecting with other local businesses and customers
(3) Discounts and coupon messaging
(4) Social Media integration with Location Based Technology
(5) Pushing local updates and notifications inside a store
(6) Greater integration between digital and physical navigation
(7) Delivery services.

Obviously, there are concerns with the protection of people's privacy, just like it always is with social media. As such, the onus is on Marketers to obtain permission from customers and take great initiative to keep them comfortable and safe, not scare customers away from utilising this technology for their convenience.

The Importance Of Peer-To-Peer Online Reviews In Marketing

The internet is like a tsunami in the ocean. While it's easy to assume that it is the result of a technological surge or some sort of digital phenomenon, in reality, it's driven by people, and despite what an organisation may try to do to resist, the wave cannot be stopped. Customers are consuming information millions of times a day searching for content, browsing for information and hunting for reviews, and the access given by platforms, portals, websites and apps are all merely surfboards in facilitating these interactions.

According to BrightLocal's Local Consumer Review Survey in 2014, 88% of people search for online reviews to determine the quality of a business. This means that, despite expensive advertising and mainstream marketing efforts, customers are still taking the word of complete strangers to assist them in forming an opinion over most other communication methods. The younger generation of Marketing professionals appreciate this, as they've grown up with this being an integral part of their lifestyle, however the older generations still unfortunately undervalue the power this type of content has on customers.

In the same survey, it was found that 87% of people also trust online reviews as much as a personal recommendation; a statistic which has grown in the last four years from 40%! This is a phenomenal shift in the way that people are utilising the internet when making purchasing decisions.

Consumers are driving this shift. They are quickly changing the way they inform themselves via the internet, and Marketing must learn to adapt in order to utilise this medium effectively by encouraging reviewing systems, promoting testimonials and enabling brand advocacy. It's a positive thing for industries, as it simultaneously provides a free PR campaign that is often far more powerful than any kind of paid advertising, and keeps organisations accountable for their products and services.

After all, according to the Harvard Business Review 2013, 57% of decisions are made by customers before they have even made contact directly with an organisation!

This is why a lot of organisations, such as RateMyAgent.com.au, ProductReview.com.au and Zomato.com.au have spawned- to create an accessible platform where people can log in and even use their own social media accounts to offer their feedback, which others are very willing to read and trust.

With this comes the obvious legitimacy issue. Reviews must be truthful and genuine, otherwise they can backfire on the organisation. Interestingly enough, consumers have developed a natural instinct when selecting and interpreting reviews. The new culture sees people read all ranges of reviews and then naturally dismiss silly, unwarranted, fake or even old feedback, and seek out the legitimate ones.

Peer-to-peer reviews are increasingly becoming the most trusted source of information on the internet when it comes to an organisation's products. It's therefore essential for Marketing to not only encourage and manage these, but also ensure that the product deserves its positive reviews, and then promote such reviews to other potential customers in order to capitalise on this medium. This kind of crowd-sourcing is relatively inexpensive and very powerful in creating a strong brand-advocacy message.

The Only Thing You Deserve In Life Is An Opportunity

Are you whinging or are you winning in business?

It's a rough, tough business world out there! Yet some succeed while others fail. So how do you and your organisation stay afloat?

The only thing every individual in business (and life, for that matter) deserves is an opportunity; the rest is completely up to us! They come by several times a day, so are you taking advantage as much as you can? As much as you'd like? Or are you making excuses?

Don't say "one day." Do it right now with what you have and improve along the way. Starting the ball rolling is always better than waiting for the so-called perfect time, because a year from today, your future-self will wish that you had have started today.

Be a 'purpose driven' organisation and move forward, not for perfection but for advancement. No one person or business is ever perfect, and everyone needs to grow and learn, but you can't hide away until you've read every resource available; there comes a point where you need to keep moving and gain real-world experience.

And with that, some things succeed, and others fail. However, true success is all about your ability to absorb failure. You can't be afraid of making choices and running with it; it's better to head in a direction and learn from victories and losses, than remaining in neutral.

It all comes down to what you and your organisation really want to do. Are you going around in unfulfilling circles? Or are you proudly endeavouring every day with a solid mission? The problem is, many people and organisations have no idea what that looks like, so a better way to discover your ideal path is about knowing what you don't want. When you rule out what you dislike and what the business wants to steer clear of, you will often uncover what you do want.

In the end, remember: truly successful people always hold two ironclad beliefs:
(1) Tomorrow can be even better than today
(2) You have the ability to make that so.

Dealing With Negative Online Reviews

In a digital world where everything is shared and spread online via every portal and social media site in existence, reviews and feedback are floating around everywhere, at every minute, at almost every location. Some of these are constructive, cheerful and positive, and an effective organisation views these as a fantastic form of free publicity.

However, not everyone is nice online. Every single person and organisation has a hater out there, no matter what he, she or they do! It's quite a harsh world, especially in the digital sphere where most of the time, the people leaving comments don't even have to identify themselves, thus removing the risk and fear of repercussion when posting. And with social media now a staple in society, more emotionally charged customers are taking to these platforms to let companies know exactly what they think, whether it's justified or not.

Regardless of our opinions about negative feedback and reviews, especially within the business world, they are there none-the-less. Learning to deal with them in the optimal way is an ideal approach to ensure that the feedback is acted upon professionally to ensure they are not derailing your organisation by spreading the wrong message to your potential customers. After all, people trust another person's review on a product or website far more than they do any other form of marketing.

So here are a few tips:

1. If a website or social media portal allows you to take a negative comment down, do it.

While some may disagree, often it's best to delete the comment and address the person privately. This way, you avoid a horrible comment right in the middle of a page where your business is expecting a high amount of traffic, and you can assess the legitimacy of the comment. After all, you don't want potential customers dwelling on it, especially if it's not fair.

2. Respond to every complaint and negative feedback

Regardless of if you delete the comment, choose to keep the complaint public on a website or social media platform, or you have no way of removing it, it must be responded to. Most of these sites allow for a right of reply, so spend time crafting a personal, positive response to address the issue and tackle it head on. It's very important that regardless of how nasty the post is, that you do not meet fire with fire- remain professional and show other customers that you are addressing whatever the concern of the poster is. Usually, you'll find that the writer was just venting and has calmed down by the time you reply (and may even apologise or remove the comment themselves), or are happy just to be noticed and respected. It may even be the right opportunity to thank them for the feedback, should it make you aware of a weakness in your organisation.

3. Keep your eye on other external websites

There are many external websites, like Trip Advisor, True Local, Rate My Agent and Yelp that are literally portals facilitating all reviews by the public. Even though a business usually cannot directly impact or run their own page on those sites (or have limited control), it's best to keep an eye out for negative comments so you are addressing concerns from these customers out in the market, beyond your own websites. Then, as in step two, if there is a right of reply (which there usually is), craft a response and deal with the issue.

4. Don't take comments personally

In a business world, things must remain professional, even if the person leaving feedback is making their comment a personal attack. Often, you will not know the real reason behind their comment and so, again, address the post positively and open up a dialogue so that you can be seen to be correcting the problem and at the same time, taking it on board. Offer your customer a public apology for their negative experience, or you may even believe that compensation may be justified in certain cases. It's best to use your own careful judgement- don't admit to fault unless you really are at fault!

6. Not all negativity is bad

If you are continually receiving the same complaint, or some of the feedback really is ringing true, perhaps it's time to review that part of your business to work out why. Sometimes the negative feedback isn't just people being petty- there may be a legitimate concern that you should be addressing in the way you do business. Keep tabs on the legitimate cases and perhaps seek to improve or act upon the feedback to stem the tide and bring things back to a positive for your customers.

Dealing with online negativity and customer complaints is never a simply task, however instead of viewing them all as an intimidating and daunting inevitability, instead, try seeing it as an opportunity for improvement. Acting in a calm and professional way will see your organisation shine, no matter the type of review you're receiving, and let's hope that the positive ones continue to outweigh the negatives!

Ensuring Your Content Is Engaging, Relevant and Fresh

Are you, like most Marketing professionals, in amongst the storm of creating content to help promote your brand and organisation, yet struggling to keep your potential and loyal customers coming back for more? You're not alone. After all, if people aren't following your content and feeling enlightened by it, then it really is a waste of time.

So here are some quick tips to keep you on track.

(1) Rule Of Correspondence

First things first. Does the content you're producing have any relation to the brand, product or organisation you're pairing it with? The whole rationale behind content is tying it in with a common theme or goal. For example, if you are a charity, then your regular content should revolve around interesting updates, wins and success stories that have been achieved due to the funds received. This engages and rewards current donators and inspires others to donate in the future. If you are a hardware warehouse, then content about DIY projects and newly stocked items is the way to go, so as to attract interested customers into your store and try building things with your products themselves.

See the trend here? Your content should work alongside your organisation and branding goals to bolster them, while at the same time, offering the reader an incentive to interact with it. Win Win.

(2) Stay Relevant

This means, your writers are keeping abreast of trends and what's hot at the current moment. No one seeks content that is boring or out of style- people want new and on-topic items that benefit them by consuming it now. So mention relevant news items or emerging styles that tie in with your brand or organisation. For example, if you are a car manufacturer, mention the latest safety technology in your models, or interesting tips about what fuels to avoid.

There are other benefits to this. Releasing content about upcoming products will provide fantastic market intelligence given how your audience responds. That way, you can tweak your product lines to suit how customers are reacting to your press releases.

(3) Make It Personal

People today can easily spot the real from the fake. Your content should be genuine and highly aligned with the values of your organisation and brand. Keep the tone personal and tell a good story which encapsulates your message in a fascinating way which is highly tailored to your audience, rather than a boring white paper document that doesn't resonate with them at all. Customers want to feel unique and loved, so cater your marketing content right to them.

(4) Keep It Interesting

An obvious one- hook them in! Keep the content simple, sharp and above all, interesting! You're wasting your time if no one is drawn in and consuming your content from the get-go. So, it's best to begin with a clever hook or thought-provoking question that begs them to read on and, thus, gets your message across. You want the reader to have learned something by the end and feel like that time wasn't wasted.

(5) Facilitate Feedback and Sharing

Don't just release one-way content. Finish with a question which opens the floor and allows for comments and opinions- even the negative ones. And never forget to allow people to share your content to their own social media platforms. Your Marketing efforts will gain a far better reach if you allow your readers to engage, reply and spread it everywhere for you. Make it as easy as possible for them to take it and run, and you'll get far more out of each post than you'll even imagine!

And, extra points for continuing to weigh in on the comments after the original content has been posted. People love to know that their contribution has been acknowledged, so join the conversation (politely)!

(6) Mix Up The Mediums

Adding photos and videos, GIFs and audio to the content mix greatly improves its appeal. Vary it up and make it really easy for people to interact with it. No one likes the same thing over and over, so offer them visual and audio cues to go along with your content. It makes it far more inviting and will encourage engagement.

(7) Regular Posts

Don't leave people waiting, but don't over-saturate either. Find a nice balance, relevant to your industry and customer profile and then deliver consistently. You want your audiences looking forward to your next release or at least pleasantly surprised when your new post pops up in their feed. Reward them for their loyalty.

Getting Copywriting Right

Getting your content right is so important! Actually, it's vital.

Sub-standard writing reflects poorly on you, your brand and your organisation. The savvy consumer of today can spot the difference, and your competitor will quickly out-class you. So spend the time perfecting your writing style and technique (or hire an amazing copywriter, who specialises in these kinds of things) so you always look amazing to your target audience! Earn their respect with your content and you'll be seeing success in no time!

Are You Asking Your Customers Too Much?

Is the customer always right? That really is the question... but in today's digitally surging and rapidly changing environment, does this still stand true?

Remember the episode of The Simpsons where Homer designs a car based on what he, as the average American, wants? Or when Kraft's new Cheese Vegemite product ended up with the horrific customer-voted name of iSnack2.0? Both were absolute disasters, and illustrate the point that a lot of Consumer Psychologists and Market Researchers are wrestling with at the moment with product and brand innovation: whether or not to ask their customers for their advice when it comes to product decisions.

If you have ever transformed a brand, re-branded or repositioned a product, you'll understand how tough this can be in general, especially when emotionally charged customers want to have a say. That old adage of 'the customer is always right' certainly holds true to a degree, but the world has changed and evolved quite a bit since those simple 'selling equals money' days. With the new-age customer being highly informed and presented with an abundance of choice, not to mention countless avenues of feedback, do they *really* know what they want?

Consumers Cannot Express Or Predict Their Needs

Consumers are statistically quite unable to explain motivations behind their behaviours, and even worse at predicting how they will act in certain situations or to new offers. Research has shown that the bias levels and inaccuracy involved is incredibly high because they struggle to understand their own rationales which then leads them to overthink when presented with a new product or campaign. So basing product and organisational decisions on their responses alone is not as reliable as one would think.

This is why market research is such a detailed and extensively scientific process; because it has to ask the right questions in order to break through these biases to find the real truth underneath. So, while the consumer may say one thing, it may be several complicated underlying factors which *really* leads them to a conclusion, and thus they didn't even know that was happening inside their 'consumer black box'.

There are many ways of getting valuable consumer insight, and unfortunately, asking them what they think or want is rarely one of them.

People Dislike Loss

Marketers today are quite familiar with the concept of loss aversion, whereby a loss is felt with around twice the intensity of a relatively equal gain. So when evolving a brand, definitely take this into consideration. Marketers must manage this by being discrete about product removals, or providing substantial justification so that customers learn to deal with it (or morn) in their own time, rather than going to the shelves and finding it missing.

Sovereignty Of Customer Choice

We all yearn for autonomy; a sense that we are in total control of the decisions we make. People hate the 'slimy sell', where they feel they are being manipulated or guided into ways of buying and using a product, rather than discover it themselves. Customers prefer to come to their own conclusions, so if you are altering your strategy or repositioning, make the changes and *then* let the consumer make their decisions afterward, not before.

Customer Opinions Are To Be Taken Lightly

Managing consumer-shock at product changes is one of the greatest challenges facing marketers today. Consumers thrive on consistency, like things to be kept simple, and are not shy anymore about voicing their opinions, too! They prefer tweaks not revolutions, and they want us to downplay change, especially to brands they have a strong advocacy to.

Marketers need to carefully manage the feedback and opinions offered by their customers and take this data into careful consideration, rather than gospel. After all, some of the most revolutionary niches were realised when the initially sceptical customer discovered a new found love for the new product.

This is clearly seen with a lot of Apple's early products, such as the iPod. Steve Jobs was famous for ignoring what customers thought, and instead, told them what they wanted, to great success.

Do Customers Still Want Things For Free?

It's quite a bold title and suggests quite the paradox.

Free is always good, and as modern customers, we want (and sometimes expect) free everything! However, has the "cost" of free become too much for people now?

There's no such thing as a free lunch- it's a sentiment as old as time itself, however it still holds as true as gravity. In a business model, if someone is getting something free, then another party is footing the bill. Over the last five or so years, organisations have found the 'free', multi-sided platform very innovative and effective, turning traditional ways of conducting transactions on its head.

In a free business model, a substantial customer segment continually benefits from a free offer, which is financed by another part of the model or customer segment. For example, RealEstate.com.au is a platform which lists properties for sale and rent for people to browse and apply for free of charge, instead charging the Real Estate Agencies to place their properties on display.

The most popular and captivating of these models, however, is the 'Freemium', which is where you get the basics for free and pay for the full version. Often, the free offer is offset by featuring paid advertising which is displayed to users as they use. It's quite effective when marketing Smartphone apps and software to the masses because there's no risk to the customer to give the product a try, therefore maximising uptake, and then once they enjoy the features, they will continue to use it. This leads to either revenue from advertising or users paying for the full version. Now, whilst customers were quite content enjoying the free versions for years, they are starting to change their behaviour.

Take Spotify, the popular music streaming service, as an example. It offers users free access to almost all music tracks, artists and podcasts on demand, right at their fingertips. It's free to use if you don't mind the occasional advert here and there between your playlists. Or even YouTube, which provides free access to endless amounts of video content for you to watch and get lost amongst, but be prepared to sit through adverts at the start and pop-up banners during.

That's all well and good, however with the saturation of adverts across all of these platforms moving in and really pushing the limits of customer experience and usability, the market trends are starting to shift again. People are beginning to see the value in ad-free subscriptions so they can gain all the benefits of the product without the interruptions and distractions of ads. So instead of just putting up with loud, jarring advertising in-between a customer's music streaming at the gym, they're now electing to pay the monthly subscription to gain the premium benefits.

This is an interesting shift for Marketing, as only years before, the customer was being pleasantly surprised by receiving effectively a service for nothing. It caught marketers and organisations off guard as it was revolutionary to not charge customers for a product. Most digital products and some innovative physical ones allowed for this paradigm shift, and it was highly profitable, however after years of this, the average person is becoming fed up with the extrinsic, non-monetary costs associated with their free use, and organisations are now seeing a demand for ad-free versions. This means that the typical modern customer who is quite accustomed to not paying, is now learning to pay again because the 'cost of free' is lowering their utility.

What a crazy, confusing and logically defying statement! Never-the-less, it's happening.
Truth be told, it's not like the cycle has exactly reversed to how things were before the free trend; all industries are seeing an advancement in the way customers interact and use these products. For example, with music, it's not like people are going back to paying $30 for a physical CD again. The overall market and the way a customer consumes music went from being free to now subscription-based, ad-free streaming. This seems to be the new and highly accepted trend now, which is being embraced all over the world.

There has also been a rise in ad-blocker software which is another threat to the Freemium model, especially on social media platforms such as Facebook or Youtube, as these 'cheating' customers are receiving all of the benefits for free without having to 'pay' the trade-off of adverts.

It's an interesting trend, and it will be even more interesting to see where innovative thinkers will take organisational models to next.

Has Wearable Technology Become Daggy?

For years now, the smartphone and tablet have become undeniable pillars in modern society, and with emerging new advancements in the App and telecommunications space, these devices have well-engrained themselves as must-have staples. People from across the globe can do endless, customisable things with their phones and tablets, and they absolutely love it.

Then, 2015 saw the biggest uptake of something new: wearable technology, mostly in the form of the smart wristwatch. Samsung and Apple raced to get their competing versions out, offering the next big thing in the form of an advantageous extension to the smartphone. It was trendy, exciting, innovative and damned-right futuristic! Due to sci-fi movies, we'd been waiting for this day for years!

So, upon their release, the hype was absolutely huge. The typical line of campers congregated outside of the Apple Store Fishbowl on George Street, Sydney around the block, and initial stock was limited. No one could wait to get their wrists on one and flash it around for everyone else to see.

However, I feel that what was once a respectable and awe-striking sight to see polished metal poking out of someone's sleeve has, one year later, become extremely daggy. That high-powered executive who, at the start of the meeting announced, "Please silence all mobile phones... and (winks while pulling his shirt cuff back) watches," once a hero, is now the laughing stock of the office. I guarantee that, in the office place today, he or she never mentions their Apple watch and keeps the wearing of it extremely subtle. Even all of my Apple iZombie friends who originally dashed out to buy one now leave it lying in a sock draw. Oh, and I haven't caught a glimpse the highly unique design of a Samsung Watch since 2014!

Even at the gym, what used to be a sea of FitBits on every wrist in yoga class is now the odd one or two. So what happened? Are customers becoming less enthralled by this kind of device? Has the novelty worn off

---

so much that customers are now almost averse to what's currently available?

I attended a conference last year where Doctors were claiming that health data-collection provided by wearables like the FitBit and Jawbone was going to be the next big step in medical care and patient treatment. GPs were convinced that they would be able to integrate their patient's FitBit stats into their diagnosis and regular check-ups. It sounded amazing in theory. However, if you're anything like my dad in his sixties, who is the ideal target-market for what these Doctors were talking about, he literally scolded me for even considering the fact that he'd ever wear one.

Even the new Samsung VR mobile wearable which places your mobile phone into a goggle-like device, creating a 3D Virtual Realty headset seems to be struggling. Samsung were initially giving these sets away only if you pre-ordered the new Galaxy S7 handset in January, however I heard an advert this week on the radio announcing that all S7s now come with it, free. It seems that they can't even give them away. And let's be honest, if you've seen what they look like, I guarantee that, like the joystick or the Gameboy Printer, the VR will be the device that our future-selves in a couple of years will look back at and laugh.

It goes to show that, right now, both the customer and corporation have no idea what we all really want from technology at the moment.

Don't be mistaken- wearable technology has a lot of space to grow and will become a highly performing sector over the next few years, but perhaps what we have now has come and gone. Current tech watches seem to have outlived their novelty and utility, and both customers and organisations are looking forward to even better manifestations, like tech clothing, smart glasses and contact lenses, advances in data capture and display, gesture-triggered interfaces and seamless wearable integration.

So despite the fact wearable technology is far from the focus of current consumer spending and admiration now, they certainly have a place in our modern world and it is inevitable that they will eventually become as ubiquitous and as loved as our smartphones and tablets. But it's not this way at the moment.

The Six Pillars Of A Complete Marketing Strategy

As a Marketing Consultant, a common question my clients ask me is: *"what are the necessary elements I should be including in my Marketing strategy?"*

Whilst the answer is not complicated on the surface, it can be quite an extensive process and require a lot of strategic planning. However, this shouldn't be avoided as you can discover a lot about your business and its identity when creating a proper Marketing Strategy.

An effective Marketing strategy needs to do six key things, all of which are interrelated:
(1) Promote
(2) Educate
(3) Attract
(4) Support
(5) Solidify
(6) Broaden

They all have to be done simultaneously in a continuous cycle, because your target customers will all be at different stages. So while one customer may be getting promoted to, the other may be being educated, and another, converted and so on.

By fulfilling and actively executing initiatives from each pillar, your business will be covering all areas of the business and communicating at all stages of the buying process. This Marketing structure is thorough and will ensure you're maximising your marketing strength to work best for you in all areas of the business.

Here is a further explanation of each pillar and some examples that your business can adopt.

First, Promote- this is all about letting potential customers know who

you are.

- Advertising and promotion
- Social Media Posts
- Business Pages
- Paid social media advertising
- Google Adwords
- Networking
- Business Partnerships

Second, Educate- now people know about you, you want to let them know you are not only knowledgeable, but a key opinion leader.

- Set up a blog on your website
- LinkedIn comments, sharing and articles
- Facebook content
- Regular content posts
- Papers and articles
- Newsletters

Third, Attract- they are keen, so now you lay down a call to action and an incentive to contact you.

- Stronger driving content plus call-to-action
- "What we do" video
- "Why choose us" video
- Value, customer-based incentives that appeal

Forth, Support- when they contact you, you need marketing to support your sales efforts.

- Pre-sale materials
- Sales Aids
- After-sale materials

Fifth, Solidify- You've made the sale or contract, now you need to retain them and keep them happy.

- Regular surveys

- Reminders and "check ins"
- Phone call scripts
- Regular surveys
- Feedback channels

Lastly, Broaden- Now it's time to get your satisfied customers to work for you.

- Customer testimonials
- Customer video
- Shareable content via social media
- Surveys and satisfaction
- Incentives for customer referrals

If your business is conducting efficient and effective marketing tactics at each pillar, then congratulations! You have a solid Marketing approach and will be experiencing amazing results! If not, then perhaps you need to work out where your tactics may not be as effective as they could be and bolster each pillar so the whole marketing strategy is working for your business.

Marketing Is Important, Right From The Start

One of the worst things an organisation of any size and purpose can do is to underestimate the compulsory nature of Marketing.

Have a good think about your own business- are you guilty of this?

Marketing is one of an organisation's most essential resources! It's absolutely crucial you get it right from the beginning because Marketing really is the backbone of an organisation. Think about it: your Marketing plan determines an organisation's name, branding, tone, imagery, positioning, tactics, strategy, approach, customer target, communication method, product range, pricing, service offering, distribution network, and so on.

Read the above again- it sounds like Marketing really defines the entire business, doesn't it? That's because it does!

The biggest mistake any organisation can do is to "just start" without giving even a little bit of thought to Marketing. You don't want to start designing products without defining what your target market actually want first; this dates back to very early business principles from the 80ies. We're in the 2010s now and you won't survive! Nor do you want to create a selling kit to give to your team without considering the organisation's identity, messaging, tone or branding. Could you imagine how ad-hoc and sporadic your social media accounts will look to your customers without a cohesive message or plan behind it all? You'll end up looking like you're running a teenager's profile, as opposed to a professional business.

It's essential to map out your overall Marketing Plan from day one so that the organisation is streamlined, effective and efficient when operating, because there is nothing more destined to fail than an uncoordinated business.

The world is too small and your competitors, too many and too smart for you to not take the market place seriously. Don't leave your total Marketing,

Content and Communications strategy up to chance, and more importantly, don't do it by piece-meal, as this will lead to a non-cohesive plan which, in-turn, will confuse your customers and waste your resources; something no business can afford to do.

Marketing is a beast worth taking the proper time and investment to nurture, as you'll reap the benefits very quickly. Conversely, if you neglect or fail to give it the right attention, it can be devastating just as fast. Trust me, it's not something you want to find out from first-hand experience.

As a Marketing Consultant, something every one of my clients say is: "I wish I had have done more with Marketing earlier on." The longer you leave it, the harder it becomes to reverse the damage and get fixed!

Don't underestimate the power of Marketing! And if you feel that you're out of your depth with the whole thing, it's worth the investment to hire a consultant to map it all out with you. You'll thank yourself and them very quickly.

Eating That Marketing Elephant

There's no doubt about it. Marketing is changing so rapidly that it's almost becoming an impossible evolving enigma. Gone are the days when all that was needed was to print a pretty picture onto a page and show it to a mass audience to get them to come to you.

Today, we have an ever-growing list of new and expanding Marketing tactics, including:

- automation
- smart phone applications
- augmented reality
- Conversion rate optimisation
- Big Data
- live streaming
- blogging
- digital
- social media
- neuromarketing
- retargeting
- SEO
- content management
- tracking pixels
- post boosting
- sponsored listings
- adwords
- relationship
- viral

And the list goes on and on... and on.

So it's no wonder why Marketers these days are immersed *and* overwhelmed; it's both an exciting time to be in the profession, but also a daunting one. Every Marketer should always strive to be on the cutting edge of our practice, however there are only so many hours in the day! It's like you need a clone of yourself to be doing the day-to-day, while you sit and study every new technique invented that week, just to keep up!

It really is up to us, as Marketers, to keep ahead.

Naturally, not everything that pops up is always relevant, effective or useful, but a lot of it is, and as Marketing professionals, we are solely responsible for keeping up to date with our craft. It's not only that it's expected of us- we also expect it of *ourselves too*. I practise many forms of Marketing every day and employ different tactics all of the time, however I always get that one client emailing me, asking if I know what some new XYZ is and how can we use it in the new campaign. It's extremely embarrassing when you have to admit to both yourself and them that you have never heard of this XYZ they speak of!

The only way to truly keep up to date with these new techniques is to subscribe to journals and Marketing blogs to at least be made aware of what's new and upcoming, and then take the time to research and perhaps even adopt them if they fit. But- granted- it's a *mammoth* task.

So how do we deal with this?

We're only human after all, and if your role is anything like mine, you're already stretched pretty thin keeping up with your own Marketing projects, let alone investing time everyday learning what new product Facebook has introduced to help better track your ad spend or what paper is being released on a new approach to neuromarketing. It's very easy to get overwhelmed.

Worse still, Marketers tend to be results and project driven, which means we want to implement several different things which all sound amazing, and we want it done *yesterday*... and in doing so, we find ourselves in a stressed mess on the floor.

There's hope! It's one bite at a time

It really comes down to that good old cliché: how do you eat a (marketing) elephant? One bite at a time. It truly is the only way to keep abreast of the profession and hold your sanity in check. One of the best pieces of advice I give to colleagues and clients is: of a list of 30 new marketing tactics, pick two or three that are most relevant to your organisation, and get them right *first,* before looking at the next thing.

If you do that, then you're already winning! It means that you're already ahead of the game, and doing it well. It's better to focus on getting a few approaches up and running strongly and reaping solid results, than spreading your efforts poorly across too many projects at once and failing across the entire board.

For example, it would be overwhelming to adopt a massive new Marketing Automation Platform like Marketo into a new business while at the same time, implementing a new Marketing to Sales support system. Sure, both would be valuable, and perhaps there will be some overlaps, however your resources and focus will be so divided that you'll end up with an under-cooked and ineffective version of both. It's best to assess which few tactics best align with your overall Marketing Strategy and utilise your assets into launching those specific programs well to produce tangible results.

No organisation's Marketing is ever perfect, but you will certainly be pushing it in the right direction by not becoming inundated, but by being selective and open to new technology and approaches as they come available.

Ten Tips To Survive Subjective Opinions

Everyone knows that Marketing and Copywriting are subjective fields. Sure, we put a scientific strategy behind every execution, and every tactic has a measurable outcome, but in the end, it's a creative role and with it will forever come praise, subjective opinions and criticism.

How one Marketer, copywriter and designer addresses a brief will be very different to how another does, and it can be a topic of hot debate as to which approach is the right one. If you've ever had a few creative agencies pitch for your business, you will know this to be absolutely true, and there's nothing more fascinating than seeing what each creative professional or team brings to the table.

Marketing Is An Art

This is the true essence of Marketing and content creation: it's essentially an art form. It's a creative and beautiful pursuit! Most people enter into these fields because it's a way to mix their passion of creativity within a corporate or business setting, and some of the work these artists produce is inspiring. However, it's a tough gig, too! There's no textbook to guide us through each project; our clients demand fresh and innovative solutions for each unique circumstance, and while they need you to build it, they have their own ideas in mind too.

There in-lies the difficulty we Marketers often face: subjectivity.

There's always someone footing the bill or in-charge of the project, and this is where it can get complicated. It's a very delicate balance. This is not to say that either the Marketer or client is right or wrong, but that's exactly the point! When a creative execution is presented, who makes the call about what tweaks or re-envisioning should be accepted versus rejected?

Is it the client, who possesses superior knowledge and experience about their industry, business, organisation, customer and product? Or is it the trained and professional marketer? It's a tricky one, and every situation is different. Sometimes the client may be blinded to thinking outside of the norm, and therefore the Marketer needs to stand strong that their presentation is, in fact, the best solution. But other times, it may be that the Marketer doesn't fully appreciate the complexity or context of the issue, and the client must step in- or something in between.

So, if you are a creative in the business world, whatever your speciality, you must learn to manage this subjectivity. It can be hard, as creative people put their heart and soul into building their project, whether it be an article, an advert, a campaign, etc; it can feel like a personal attack when a client or colleague dislikes your solution.

Then how do we remain professional and strengthen our integrity, while pleasing our clients at the same time?

Here are some tips to manage this subjectivity:

(1) Ask a lot of questions at the start

Before running off and creating your masterpiece which you're sure your client will love, ask a tonne of questions at the very beginning. The more relevant information about the situation you have, the better. Often, the client will respect you more for asking, and you will uncover crucial facts that they didn't originally think were important to discuss with you, or simply missed.

(2) Don't present to them until you're 100% ready

We all have deadlines, but as creatives, we all have a strong gut instinct, too. We know when our work is lacking or lazy, just like we know when we are particularly proud of it too. Be 100% certain and confident in your presentation before going to the client, so that you present the best face to them.

(3) Bring a team member as backup

It can be quite intimidating when it's just you in front of a board of judgemental clients waiting for your presentation. So, if possible, perhaps consider bringing a co-worker, co-creator, or colleague to help you explain it and give you a sense of reinforcement.

(4) It's all in the sales pitch

Don't just fling printed and digital files at your client. Guide them through each execution and pitch it to them, including your thought process and how you arrived at the final product. Most clients don't specialise in content and marketing, so it's up to you to show them why it's the best solution for them.

(5) Create a few different versions, where possible.

If a client or management team are expecting a solution to a fairly complicated brief, sometimes it's best to present them with a few different options, rather than just one. This will mean that they can see how you've approached the execution, and can then interpret the differences, while choosing their favourite elements of each. This keeps you in control, because you can guide them far better with a few, than with only one. Obviously, don't go overboard, as too much choice can over complicate the process and make it more difficult for you to manage the client in the end; but three options is generally a good number.

(6) Give them time to consider

Don't rush them into an answer. As I said, it's subjective. Allow them to digest your creative, take it away and ponder it, gather different opinions and come back to you. You may also want to leave the room and let them talk amongst themselves or mull it over, without worrying they will offend you. It will produce far purer evaluations which will help you meet their expectations better.

(7) Take their feedback on board

Very important! Do not get defensive. After all, whether they are a paying client, a colleague or a friend, you must always act professional. Sure, you may be a trained artist, writer or marketer with years of experience and many qualifications, but in the end, you are presenting to them and you need to be respectful of their opinions and advice.

(8) Stand your ground

In saying that, have faith in your work. As mentioned above, you have a natural gut instinct about your work, so while you can take comments, know when to defend your idea and professionally explain why the way you've done it is best. This is quite an advanced skill, and worth honing.

(9) Accepting that the first draft will never be the final

No one should go into a first presentation believing that their first creation is going to be the final one. There will always be tweaks and customisations, so the sooner you accept this, the better you will deal with the whole process. Evaluate which changes and recommendations are best and then hit the edit button.

(10) Pick the right client

This is a tricky and controversial one , but for the sake of your sanity, it really is important to choose the right client, just like they need to choose the best creative. While not every marketer has this luxury, it's better to spend your creative energy and flair on clients who you respect and respect you, as opposed to someone who is going to micromanage, or scrap everything you do and essentially insist they do it themselves.

How To Prolong The Strength Of Your Content

In pretty much every industry and across every field, people and organisations alike are producing content in its endless forms. Blogs, videos, articles, posts, publications, books, podcasts, and the list goes on, but the single uniting goal of them all is to reach an audience for a desired purpose.

That's how content creation works today.

Everyone has this fundamental knowledge almost down pat by now, because thousands of pieces of content shoot off every day. There are close to 10,000 tweets entering the digital superhighway every second of the day, and everyone personally witnesses how quickly their LinkedIn and Facebook feeds scroll by every minute.

So with these kinds of statistics flying by at alarming rates, how are we ensuring that our precious time spent developing well-written pieces of content for our target audience is not a complete waste of time?

The answer lies in ensuring that you prolong the strength of each execution! Once the material is of the highest quality it can be, it's then all about extending its shelf life!

Here's how:

(1) Make A Big Bang The First Time

Everyone loves a brand new post, and truth be told, this wave generally receives the biggest inflow of eyeballs. That's because it's fresh and on-topic, and your most active followers will be quick to jump on, interact and respond. The goal is to ensure that this content is being promoted across all of your platforms and portals at the most high-traffic times of the day so that it's engaging the right people.

(2) Make It Easy To Share

Promoting your own content is good. Having your audience advocates share it to their networks is even better. It's the equivalent to good word-of-mouth as people trust their friend's recommendation over that of the writer alone.

So ensure that they can! Place tasteful social media share buttons and easy to copy hashtags and URLs, so when a reader decides they like your piece enough to pass it on, they can do it in an instant. This greatly extends the life of your post if it's working its way around the digital neighbourhood and becoming viral.

(3) Re-Share The Content A Few Times

Studies show that after the first launch, it's safe to assume 90% of your target audience will have unfortunately missed it. But that's ok! Studies also show that after the initial peak of readers, re-sharing the post within a reasonable time frame will rekindle the views on it, because you're casting the net out again to capture the people who more than likely simply missed your first wave. This is quite an easy method of prolonging the strength of precious content, and yet so many creators fail to do it. If you've written high quality content which is still relevant at different times, then re-sharing it will ensure it reaches the people who failed to be around at the time you posted last time.

Just a warning- don't saturate each channel by going overboard with this, as that can frustrate them, which is counterproductive.

(3) The Marketing Rule Of Three

An oldie, but a goodie. The rule of three states that when you produce one piece of content, you should be utilising it in at least three different forms to ensure maximum utilisation. We are all time poor- both creators and consumers alike- and so we want to ensure that we are not wasting precious resources failing to make the most out of our efforts. So, that blog post you wrote last month- get some recording gear and make a podcast channel discussing your original posts and the comments that resulted. Then print the article in a book, or submit it to a journal, or film it. This means that your content is working hard across several mediums and reaching those precious audience members who may perhaps prefer different ways of reading it that your original post.

(4) Use Statistics To Branch Off Into Related Content

Always back your content with a way to track it to gain some insight into how well it's being received by you audience. In today's digital world, it's a pretty simple thing to do. All social media sites offer some sort of system to see how many impressions and clicks your posts have received. The same goes with websites, video portals and podcast downloads. Having these kinds of facts and figures means you can see which piece is receiving the most attention, and then create 'spin off' content with a similar topic to get the best resonance out of your audience.

How Do You Extend The Life Of Your Content?

The above are just a few tips on how to ensure that your precious pieces of marketing content are getting the greatest penetration for the longest amount of time. After all, in business, we need to aim for maximum effectiveness at the maximum efficiency, to ensure that our content is lasting the distance. After all, it's is vital to achieving your goals over the long term.

The Overlooked Benefits Of Refreshing Your Resume

Personal resumes, or Curriculum Vitae (CVs) are such a vital commodity in today's busy business world. They are essentially the main selling device for *you* to provide to an organisation which are potentially seeking to pay you to lend them your skills in amongst a crowd of other applicants.

In a world that is so rapidly changing and experiencing such volatile economic landscapes, people underestimate the importance of regularly keeping their resumes up-to-date so that, should something occur, your back-up plan is ready to go without too much of a shocking lapse to your life. Regular updating of your resume is more important than most people probably place value in, and will unfortunately only realise when it is too late. This article is to bring to light and motivate everyone to place more importance on this by showing you the benefits.

The Importance Of Keeping Your Resume Up To Date

Not to put a depressing rationale behind this article, but as mentioned, with the ever changing and rapidly shifting state of all industries in every country throughout the world, there is a direct flow-on effect which impacts heavily on the employment market in every country.

How often do we all see in the newspaper *"4000 jobs downsized and cut by Organisation XYZ to improve profitability and create a leaner structure going forward"*? Unfortunately, more often than we, as employees, would like. An organisation is a business that functions to achieve its goals, and an inevitable reality is that they must act in such a way to remain solvent and competitive in an increasingly saturated and competitive market. Therefore, in the event that something should happen suddenly to your employment, having your resume ready to go simply makes perfect sense. It takes very little time to update and (more importantly) improve it every couple of months, and the benefits, even on a personal pride level, far outweigh the costs. It is baffling how complacent people can become in this regard, especially when they have been employed comfortably for quite a few years, completely underestimating how rapidly things can change and the impact it can have on their life.

Preparing For The Unexpected

Constant and stable employment is a key staple in most people's lives. Their pay cheque rolls in at the same time every month and it's used to maintain their standard of living, paying the bills, supporting their families, pursuing their interests and so on. Do people often consider the major impact to this routine if suddenly, they were found to be unemployed? Having your resume ready can mean that you are able to react quickly to minimise such a disturbance. Unfortunately, it is often a very stressful and emotional time when losing your job, and having this resume step already done can truly remove that quintessential hurdle on the road to recovery. Acting on *your* terms is always better than acting on someone else's – by this, I mean, editing your resume when you're in a safe position is always far better than updating it in a rush to desperately find a new job.

There Are Other Advantages Too!

Of course, it's not all bad. Having an up-to-date resume allows you to be able to quickly react to amazing new opportunities which may present themselves even while you are happily employed. LinkedIn as a platform itself specialises in the recruitment prospects of "passive searchers" who become tempted by job ads when not actively searching.

Being able to apply quickly with your impressive resume motivates you to be able to take the next step when you feel you are ready to stretch yourself in a role that will probably get snapped up quickly by thousands of others thinking the same. Be proud of your resume, and ensure to include all recent achievements and key steps which potential near-future employees will value highly.

What Do I Need To Update?

Updating your resume doesn't only revolve around putting your current employment details on it. It includes ensuring that:

- the design and fonts are consistent and modern

- you have informed your Referees that you have put their name down again for reference checks

- the contact and address details are current and conveniently located

- all recent education and relevant extra-curricular information is up-to-date

- all 'roles and responsibilities' and promotions are noted, current and relevant

Use It to Check Your Career Goals

Additionally, updating your resume can also be a great 'goal check' for you. A resume is essentially a checklist of your past and current career achievements. After you update it, you're able to personally judge your current position and open yourself up to possible areas of self-improvement that you never would have considered before. You're able to ask yourself questions like:

- Are you happy with your current position?

- Do you wish to go back and study further?

- Is there another field or industry niche you would like to try?

- What is missing from your resume that you need for the dream job?

- What remuneration package are you aiming for?

- What next steps do I need to take to achieve these goals?

All in all, whatever your motivation is for keeping your resume up-to-date, the benefits of doing so are numerous and, for the little time it takes, these benefits are all yours for the taking.

Writing Well Is What You Need

So here's the thing I was reflecting on today, and it's what I've always been told over and over by my writing mentors, author friends and even lecturers: whether it's fiction or non-fiction, basic plots, twists and ideas are easy to come by. They pop into our heads night and day (well for me they do), however this is only step one of the journey. In other words, despite most people's belief, the economy of 'the story idea' is fairly cheap.

The real key to writing success lies truly in the execution of the writing itself. Word choice, turns of phrases, paragraph length, adjectives, metaphors, similes and so on.

This means that, regardless of your plot concept and how innovative or fresh it is, the way in which you convey it and the quality of the writing style that you use will make or break you as an author or copywriter.

That's the simple truth.

In a world where books and content are in abundance, it's quality over everything else. Ideas come and go, but it's the way it's written that draws attention and effectively communicates with your reader, keeping them engaged.

An average idea written well always wins over an amazing idea written poorly. Every time.

I heard Brandon Sanderson say once that it's like listening to someone play the piano. After about 30 seconds, you can already judge how well they can play and the listener will determine if they want to stay or leave. It's the same with writing- readers invest a lot of their time into a novel or article, and if you cannot grab and reward them with quality writing, then you don't deserve their attention.

So, just like a pianist, how do you improve your writing? Practise, practise and more practise. The more you write, the better you get at it, and that way, when your perfect plot, setting, concept or idea comes along whilst you're in the shower or on the train, you have the associated skill to tell it well and be successful!

Good luck and keep at it!

Breaking News: Writing Requires Dedication

Ok, fine... so it's not so much breaking news as it is the obvious truth that people deny...

But the reality of writing is that it takes practise and dedication. LOTS of practise and dedication.

Brandon Sanderson says in his creative writing lectures: "Ideas and plots are cheap. It's the actual writing that defines the quality of the material." - and this couldn't be *more true.*

You can have the most complex setting, characters and plot, but if your articulation and expression is poor, readers will fall out of your story and find it a real punish to read. Remember, the reader is offering their time to be absorbed by your story- so you don't want to ruin your reputation and waste their time by presenting them something that is not communicating strongly with them.

The ultimate goal for a writer is to produce a work that is effortless to read, completely transporting a person beyond the pages, but you can't do that when the writing is not well-constructed and the word choice, expressive. So where does this skill come from? You guessed it! Practise.

This is why I believe "The Name Of The Wind" by Patrick Rothfuss is such an amazing, compelling and overall beautiful read. The story is communicated so perfectly by the way that he writes and describes everything. As a reader, I was utterly absorbed because the word choice was light and descriptive to allow me to be completely enthralled. However, this didn't happen overnight! Rothfuss said the reason behind it was because he wrote it so long ago, and then spent so many years polishing it that it's now "like a smoothed stone at the bottom of a running river."

It takes dedication and practise. Plain and simple.

It's all about your style and choosing your words wisely, and you get better through taking the time to get better. Want proof? If you're a writer like I am, look back at some of your earlier work. I know they say a work is never truly finished and no one ever reaches perfection, but even looking back at your drafts 6 months prior, you'll see how much you've improved if you are writing every day. I'm often horrified at some of my earlier material, but you can't beat yourself up, as just like a musician learning their instrument, the road to improvement is a necessary one.

Of course, if you enjoy it, then the process is so much easier. You won't find it a chore so much as you do a dedicated hobby.

After work each day, I go home, eat dinner and then write. I'm also a very harsh and meticulous editor, so I'll write for an hour, then go back and polish it a few times. Whilst I'm sure that's not for everyone, it helps me keep my style clean and helps me always move forward with content that I'm happy with. That way, I'm always learning from my errors and perfecting my communicative style.

Inspiration: Where Will You Be?

Inspiration- it's the vital key to everything creative that we produce, whether that manifests itself as art, music, writing, a speech, innovation, invention, and so on. It's a fuel which sparks our interest and exposes our imagination, motivating us to create.

For some, it's rare and others, not so much, but regardless, it's one of a person's most precious resources and therefore should never be squandered or wasted. Everyone one of us is unique, and when we're inspired, we create unique things. That's quite an amazing concept if you think about it.

For everyone, it varies. Inspiration may spur you into very different creative avenues to your neighbour, and that's great! Let inspiration carry your creativity! We should all let it out to play more often than we do. I've heard many stories of successful organisations making their next big breakthroughs when allowing its staff to think outside of the square and let inspiration take them somewhere they've never been before. The same goes with individuals- you only limit yourself, so the next time you feel it, harness it and see where it takes you.

Inspiration is so precious, yet most of us never know when it will strike; and therein lies the challenge! As a writer and composer myself, I understand that my muse often seems to be around when I'm in the most unlikely of places, like in the shower, nodding off in bed, on a crowded train or even on the treadmill. That's not to say that I also don't undercover it sitting at my computer, setting up to write too. My point is, when it does strike, be ready.

The beauty of modern technology is that everyone has smart phones now. So there's no excuse! Every time you hear a unique melody in your head, record it. When you have a new novel idea or plot twist, open up that phone notepad. You never know when it will happen, and it pays to be prepared. Don't be lazy- take 30 seconds to scratch down some notes. You never know what the idea may blossom into down the track.

One of the most foolish things to do when inspiration strikes, (and I know this from personal experience) is to say to yourself "this idea is awesome. I'll remember it later." Trust me, you *never* do, and then that idea is lost forever. Don't risk it!

Regardless of where or when, how or what, be prepared to listen to and make a record when creativity comes knocking. Don't forget to take advantage of that inspiration, where ever it may strike. It may produce the next Mona Lisa, the next Lord Of The Rings, the next Gettysburg Address or the next iPod.

Good luck, and stay inspired!

Taking A Break After Writing To Edit Your Work

Editing.

It's the essential step some writers hate, and therefore avoid like the plague, while others are addicted to, meaning that they can never get passed the first page. It's a tough enough process as it is, but regardless of which side of the spectrum you lie on, there is one golden rule that *always* must be followed after completing a body of work, and that's to give yourself some distance before revising your own creation.

Editing Our Work Is Crucial

Editing is so important because we aren't perfect, especially when trying to put our vision into the written word. Regardless of if you're penning a song, a text book or a work of fiction, no one ever gets it right during their first draft. But therein lies the beauty of writing: we mind-dump and brainstorm our initial ideas, and then can spend time afterward rewording, reordering and overall polishing what we've written so that when the intended audience gets the chance to read it, it's brilliant!

Of course, it's subjective as to how many times a piece of writing requires editing, and we can leave that discussion for another time, however as I mentioned above, the golden rule is to give yourself and the work a 'breather' before you attack it with a red pen.

Why Should I Take A Break Before Editing?

Simple! When you're so entrenched in a project, you can become completely blinded by the little mistakes, because you're focusing on the bigger picture. Don't misunderstand- that's *absolutely perfectly* fine! After all, in the first draft, we *want* to be shooting for the stars and producing content which is uninhibited as much as possible. That's the idea behind of the concept of 'free-writing' and NaNoWiMo: where, for a certain length of time, you don't stop writing whatever is coming out of your head, in order to overcome self-imposed mental barriers. But then, when it comes to essential editing, you want a fresh pair of your eyes; and this is only achieved by revisiting your manuscript after a break.

Edit Your Own Work First!

Naturally, people may be tempted to just give a first draft straight to another person or pay an editor, but my personal opinion is you should *always* review your own work *first* yourself before giving someone else a raw file. This is because your project is your personal vision and only you truly understand its concept and direction at that point; so to give it to someone else at such an early stage could tarnish or misconstrue the work's direction and 'spirit', because your third party editor will interpret the body of work differently to you from your rough draft, and edit it accordingly. What you get back may be not what you ever intended and could end up wasting everyone's time. It's best to look over your own work first to get it out of first draft status before giving it to someone else.

Take A Break From Your Work

So the point is: always edit your own work in the first round, and when doing so, give yourself some distance from the project before you do. How you use this break is up to you; some people may start a new book, work on something completely different, start designing the cover art, read, or stop writing altogether for a while (which I wouldn't recommend, but each to their own!). But the point is, through this distance, when you come to edit the writing after a sufficient amount of time, you will be in a far better position to see the flaws and the errors that you would otherwise have missed, simply because at the time of writing, you were too heavily invested.

The time apart will mean that you will have forgotten a lot of the intricacies of the project and can therefore view it more as a first-time reader than an author, which is advantageous for you in first draft editing.

We've All Been There!

We see it all of the time: when someone has been writing, for example, a report for weeks and then they say they've checked it 100 times, only for you to find they've spelled their name incorrectly at the very start! Or the age-old author adage: "I wrote all day and hated everything I wrote and decided I was a terrible writer, only to reread it the next day and realise it wasn't that bad." We've all been there. But it acts as evidence to support the need to take a break before editing.

Distance Is Paramount

We're only human and we get too bogged down in things to be able to edit our own work straight away. So next time you finish your poem, your manuscript, your assignment or your white paper, allow for some time to pass, take a breather, allow the work (and your mind) to "cool off", and only then should you reach for the editing cap to give it a good scrub.

After this, then you may decide to give it to a third party, but only once you're happy that you have the project complete and in a solid state before you do so.

How Much Do Your Explain To Your Audience?

So, you're writing your next creative work, and you have this genius plot device in mind which you can't wait to show the world. You know that it's complicated (all satisfying stories are, after all), but you believe that you can guide your audience through it so that, by the end, they'll love and appreciate it as much as you do.

That's fantastic! However, what's the best and most effective way of getting the reader through from start to finish without overloading or confounding them?

It's the most trickiest of balances every author faces when writing: how much do I tell my reader?

Have you read a book before and thought: "I'm completely lost"? Or on the flip slide: "well, that was obvious"? These two questions highlight the two possible extremes which can occur, and it's very important to get that balance right to ensure your book is a success. You want to bait and intrigue with titbits of information so that your audience's curiosity is peaked, but at the same time, you don't want to leave them in the lurch so that they become frustrated and fall out of your story.

This is particularly a prominent issue in the fantasy and sci-fi genres, simply due to the nature of the genre itself with the steep learning curves and foreign staples of world building, magic systems and off-world conditions.

How Do You Get Exposition Right?

While it's all well and good to say "well if you're a good writer, you just know the balance," is this really the answer? I see this comment everywhere, but who really does know? To an extent, it is subjective, and there will always be different types of readers who appreciate your work on many differing levels, but in general, how do you get exposition right?

It's something, I myself really struggle with. I always panic that I haven't left enough clues, so I over compensate, only for my alpha readers to tell me that my plot twists were too expected or I'm leading them too artificially, which sends me back to the drawing board to rewrite those early chapters.

So, from my experience, here are a few tips to help:

(1) Tend to lean more to the 'less is more' side.

I have found that it's far better to stick to keeping information and exposition to a minimum, simply because if you cut out the excessive detail, it flows better. Authors naturally put too much detail in rather than too little, so if you err to the conservative side, you're probably within the perfect balance.

(2) Your audience is smarter than you think.

Don't baby your readers! They will surprise you with how quickly they pick up the threads of your story and weave them into understanding, usually before you even expect them to. It's often hard from your author ivory tower to fully appreciate this, but it's true! Remember back to all of the books you've read and how you did the same; take this into consideration.

(3) Keep in mind you know the whole story and they don't... yet.

Often as a writer, your view is biased by the fact that you know the entire plot. You must keep this in mind when writing. Alpha and beta readers are an excellent check for this: if you find their feedback is that you, as an author, are talking down to them or pushing them through the plot device rather than letting them draw their own conclusions, you need to fix this. People read for pleasure, and you're not giving this to them by doing that.

(4) If you find you are explaining a lot, your approach is wrong.

If your plot or element is complex and you're finding yourself cramming tonnes of explanation into every chapter, then it's time to consider approaching the pacing and device in a different way. For example, the first time you introduce a unique magic system, completely show and don't tell, so the reader is impressed and their curiosity is peaked. Then, the next time, add a few hints based on an exchange between two users. And then a chapter later, have more explained by two officers attempting to catch the magic user. Then have a mentor teach a pupil chapters after this, and so on.

This kind of 'spread' approach from entirely different angles gives the reader the exhilaration of piecing together their own full picture from several different scenes, rather than a single chapter where it's explained in its entirety, which will bore or completely confuse your audience in one go.

(5) Leave room for theories.

Fans absolutely love loose ends from your stories (within reason, of course!). There are entire forums discussing every single line from your book and developing their own exciting theories as a result. This is quite exciting and fun for fans and builds hype for your next instalment, so give them that opportunity! This obviously means ensuring your writing is very tight and precise so that they can pick up your twists and subtle hints, and therefore facilitate their speculations.

(6) Don't be afraid to re-write

NO ONE gets it right the first time. EVER. Listen to the feedback you get during your first few drafts and never just settle with how it is, because as an author, you look at your work as an omnipotent storyteller with rose coloured glasses, and... in the end, it's your readers who matter most. Listen to them and get it right. Go back and review.

Getting That Balance Perfect

Again, it's a tough balance nailing encumbering your audience with exposition, and withholding too much that they become completely frazzled within the first 50 pages. Ensure that you follow the above tips, and pay close attention to your alpha and beta readers. They will help you so that your wider audience gets to truly love and appreciate your masterpiece like you intended.

What Does The Future Hold In Store For Print Marketing?

It all started with print. In the not-too-distant past, tangible inky copies of everything was how Marketing and Communications simply worked. It was the benchmark and the cornerstone of advertising, whether it was publications, banners, print advertising, white papers, sales aids, mail outs, booklets or pamphlets.

Then, the rise and exponential popularity of the internet disrupted the entire form as it was, and the whole game changed. People began to see print as boring or old-fashioned, and 'electronic-everything' was the sleek new thing.

Everyone demanded everything digitally and patience was no longer a virtue when it came to communication. Attention spans fell dramatically, and with it came a lost appreciation of tangible creativity. All we ever hear now (if it's mentioned at all!) is how dead Print Marketing is; and yet, is that *really* so?

It seems that, while the digital sphere is on the fast-track highway of innovation and gaining a lot of attention for this, clever Marketers are beginning to notice that Print still has so much to offer.

Print Media Complements Digital Assets.

One way that Print has adapted is through the integration of executions alongside digital executions. The infamous QR code allows customers to scan a physical piece of marketing which can take them to a desired (and trackable) website or social media page for further engagement.

There are more innovative executions, too. For example, in Montreal, Canada, there are printed Instagram border cut-outs at the major sites with the hashtag #MTLMoments, encouraging tourists to capture and share the beautiful attractions through the tourism hashtag, thus promoting the city for them for free.

Augmented reality is another fantastic way Print and Digital marry up. What may appear to be a regular print advert in a magazine can suddenly spring to life by placing your iPad over it, greatly increasing the advert's appeal.

Print Media Is Still Highly Engaging.

There is some truth to the 'outdated-ness' of *some* forms of print media executions, but again, that's only if your organisation is doing the same thing as companies were doing in the 70ies!

Direct mail has evolved over the years to be far more innovative in its executions. Instead of a boring formal letter, there are different styles of colourful cards which unfold before the receiver's eyes. There are digital cards that house a small screen inside which plays a video alongside a printed message when opened. There are new types of inks, including foil prints and holograms which catch the eye and ensnare intrigue. There are all different sizes, shapes and designs of envelopes designed to pique the interest of a potential client and never be forgotten. There are perfumed prints and embossing to intrigue the less-catered for senses. The possibilities are endless.

A good Marketer is able to think outside of the square and utilise Print Marketing to augment their campaigns and gain cut-through with innovative executions such as these.

Print Media Can Be Individually Tailored.

Customers today expect tailored messaging. They want their own name and catered message on everything they receive, otherwise they ignore it. This can be integrated easily today with Print Marketing, where each customer can be sent a branded catalogue which is specifically relevant to them and their interests.

I received a calendar last year from a company, and in each photo for each month, my name was integrated seamlessly into the image. For example, my name was written with pebbles on a beach for January, and in the snow for June, and so on. This simple execution meant that I used that calendar all year because it was clever and specific to me, *and* it achieved its goal of placing their brand in front of me on a daily basis.

With the onset of Marketing Automation, Print Media can be utilised just as effectively in these kinds of executions. If a website is tracking how each customer uses your website, Marketing Automation processes can be set to immediately execute highly specialised printed materials, targeted to their individuality.

Innovation Is Within Reach (and highly affordable).

New agencies, such as Dashing Print in Australia, are beginning to emerge which solely specialise in unique printing executions and groundbreaking designs. Those outlandish ideas, once considered impossible and ridiculously expensive, are now completely possible and in fact encouraged by more demanded customers today. If you want a wind-up butterfly that shoots out of an envelope when the receiver opens it, or a star shaped envelope which unfolds like a rose, these agencies specialise in making your creative concepts an affordable reality.

The sky's the limit with printing creativity. Innovation can be found even on print packaging. Coca Cola won awards for their highly successful 2013 campaign which saw cola bottles labeled with individual names. The following year, they had cola cans in all different colours, to "match with your individual personality." In 2015, their Coca-Cola brand itself changes physical colour depending on the temperature of the liquid is inside! This is an organisation that understands Print Media's importance in their Marketing campaigns, and they continue to have success with a mature product because of it.

Use Print Marketing Effectively To See Success.

Right now, it's shaping up to be an even more exciting world for Marketing, and Print Media is no exception.

Don't think of Print Marketing as a critically extinct beast, hanging on to survival by its fingertips by desperately trying to claw its way back into your Marketing campaign and budget, as that's not the reality. Instead, Print Marketing should act as an essential complement to your digital strategy.

Customers still see allure in exciting and innovative printed pieces, and therefore, they still have a place and an essential role to perform in communication.

People don't always exist in cyber-space, and humans by nature are tactile creatures. An effective Marketing campaign can be given a huge advantage by incorporating some of the more innovative Print Marketing solutions on offer that can reach your target demographic like never before.

Blending Paper With Pixels

The future of effective communication lies in combining innovative digital and print Marketing to establish a more holistic approach.

Within the current Marketing space, the focus is on digital, digital, *digital*. Social media has gone from simple peer-to-peer sharing, to a complex layering of marketing mechanics which require constant attention to tame the beast and obtain the best results. Websites and keywords are paramount, online exposure is essential, smartphone apps are the new *everything*, and relevant content is king. However, there seems to be an unfortunate neglect of an accompanying resource, and that's print marketing. Younger marketers are so entrenched within the fast-paced stupor of digital platforms that they've lost touch with the real advantages that print can offer to bolster their overall executions. The ground-breaking mix lies, not in one or the other, but in the innovative blending of the two mediums, both tangible and intangible, that truly sees a marketing campaign gain cut-through in the competitive industries of today. With everyone clambering to reach the lofty peaks of web analytics and marketing cyberspace, there is real power to be found in a strategic synergy between print and digital which can strengthen any marketing campaign quite significantly.

Bridging The Gap

Consumers spend a lot of time online; there's no denying it. However, they live in the real tangible world, and reaching them effectively requires a delicate balance of both. The ultimate strategy lies in creating a bridge between an organisation's digital assets and complementing printing pieces. This could be as simple as a website address or social media hashtag on a pamphlet or more advanced such as mobile scannable codes, smartphone augmented reality or physical proximity marketing. Creating a link between these media greatly enhances a customer's experience and reinforces an overall marketing campaign many times over, because they both have their own unique strengths and advantages. For example, print provides a sensory experience, and in an online world where everything seems fleeting to a customer, the feel of paper in the hand offers a deep connection between them and your brand in a way that digital just can't alone. It can trigger the senses and offer a whole new 'off-screen' dimension to the campaign, creating an immersive experience with your audience that, in the hands of an innovative marketer, can provide a unique freshness which elevates marketing far beyond anything else. It can then drive people to social media and website platforms to continue their customer journey towards conversion.

The Addition of Print Adds Substance

Print is so flexible that is really does make it an ideal marketing medium to support a comprehensive digital strategy because it's diverse, engaging, versatile and creative. Gone are the days of boring print; cutting-edge designs and inspirational creations is where print executions are now, and while digital clutter can often be ignored or passed over, print media offers an edge because it has a 'reserved space' in people's lives that they're fond of. For example, everyone has grown up with paper newspapers that they associate with education and credibility. Glossy magazines inspire engagement through entertainment. A direct mailing piece gains access into people's homes and lives, delivering an accessible sales message, and catalogues motivate customers to research further leading to online conversion. The list goes on, but each version fulfils a unique marketing role that can never be fully replicated by newer forms of technology. A uniform strategy which encompasses the utilisation of both together ensures that all angles are covered and can reach the potential customer in the way that they prefer.

Taking Action with Digital and Print

So, it's time for Marketers to rediscover the hidden power of print as a complement to their digital Marketing strategies, as it will provide that extra edge your organisation and brand requires within highly competitive industries.

Empowering Your Marketing Team

The creative arena of Marketing requires people who are innovative and bold, experimental and inventive. Organisations rely on their Marketing department to produce effective solutions which aren't derived from a Standard Operating Procedure or text book, and while we all understand and expect this, are we empowering our team to take risks and reach for the stars?

Why People Gravitate To The Creative Arts

It's very easy to see why people are drawn to the Marketing arenas of the business world- in an adult environment all about results and the bottom line, Marketing allows for the application of limitless imagination and creativity to bring about solutions. That's why I pursued it, and I'm sure I'm not alone!

While some may find the daily 'outside of the box thinking' as a way to earn a pay cheque quite intimidating, everyone within the Marketing arts embraces it. We enjoy the fact that there is never a standard way of doing things; every day is different and in order to be successful, we need to constantly be innovative and bold.

So while these skills are initiated and introduced when studying Marketing, they are really earned and learned on the job in a role where we can get our hands dirty.

So, how do we empower the next generation to take on the challenge?

Everyone starts from the bottom (despite what Millennials believe they're entitled to!). We've all been there, regardless of our industry or career path, and those entry level jobs consist of the obligatory support role for the rest of the Marketing department. While they are a fantastic learning platform to begin a career full of opportunity, at some point or another, we needed Marketing Management to eventually allow us to step away from the repetitive, and branch out toward the unknown.

I personally recall doing all of the admin work for my boss' product line at my first marketing job. It was great putting all of the theory I had learned from University into perspective in a real life environment, but it was the moment when I was given my own product line, albeit small, that I saw how much of a difference it was.

Once you get your first opportunity to devise your own Marketing strategy and implement your own ideas, combined with the risk of success and failure hanging in the balance, you become a completely different person: you evolve into becoming a real Marketing professional, and let's be honest, that's where we all want to be.

But there's a common hurdle...

It happens all too often in Marketing departments- the whole mantra of 'it's just better if I do it myself'. Upper management are, at times, reluctant to stretch out and give a bit of the responsibility to their more junior colleagues. It doesn't even have to be a jealousy thing- it can be just the fact that certain people like their work in a particular style, and become hesitant to put it in the hands of someone else. But therein lies the issue: we aren't empowering the next generation of creatives.

It comes down to subjectivity

This issue here is that Marketing and all of the creative fields, by their very nature, are subjective. Each person's marketing campaign and strategy is often quite different to what another would propose. While that's not a bad thing, per se, it can be a hindrance when we wish to empower our colleagues to make their own mark on our organisations.

So, what must we do? We have to empower our Marketing teams!

(1) As Marketing Management and Chief Marketing Officers, we must remember that the empowerment of our colleagues is crucial on so many levels, not least of which is for their personal career growth. Who knows where they will go, but it's good knowing that you were able to give them a leg up in the right direction.

(2) Create a safe environment, where people are allowed to take risks and make mistakes within reason. You cannot empower your team and hold them back at the same time.

(3) Involve the team in weekly meetings where everyone discusses their current projects, and then open the floor for everyone to offer ideas and suggestions.

(4) We mustn't forget that we are where we are today because someone gave us the chance at some point, and now that chance is within our power to grant. So grant it! When the next campaign comes up, invite a few different members of the team to participate.

(5) Pass on good habits and expertise to the next generation of creative professionals, so they can learn and ultimately put their own character and spin on things. New, fresh approaches are often exactly what an organisation needs to evolve.

(6) Learn to let go and outsource your never-ending to-do lists to your colleagues who you've hired to do that very thing. Stop being over-territorial and let the reigns go a little.

(7) Allocate money in the yearly budget to offsite training courses, Marketing conferences and other learning opportunities, in addition to the on-the-job learning experience. It's a big world out there; one which is constantly changing, and we mustn't get boxed into our own little worlds too much.

(8) Further to the above point, sign the team up for reputable industry magazines and institutes, such as the Australian Marketing Institute. They will appreciate the offers and updates these resources offer them and indicate that you truly care about their progression.

(9) Monitor your team and track their progress- after all, you are still the manager and must remain in control- but don't micromanage. You want to encourage a creative environment for fresh ideas.

Good luck! I hope these tips help you connect far better with your Marketing colleagues!

Postface from the Author

I hope you feel more enlightened after reading through my collection of short essays.

The Corporate Cornerstone volumes are designed as a brief collection of Marketing and Business essays for the successful business professional looking to further their knowledge. The volumes will be released regularly with fresh and informative topics.

I trust you enjoyed Volume Two of this series, and I look forward to you joining me in Volume Three.

Thank you.

Christopher Melotti
www.melottimedia.com.au